Zay's day at Basketball Camp

Written By Isaiah K. Wills

© 2021 Isaiah K. Wills. All rights reserved.

Published by Wills Family Publishing No portion of this book may be reproduced in any form without permission from the publisher, except as permitted by U.S. copyright law.

Year 2021
YOUNIVERSAL GROWTH LLC

ISBN: 9978-1-7342496-2-0

Every Saturday at 8 o'clock, my dad wakes me up in the morning so I can get ready for basketball camp. I go to a basketball training camp that helps improve my basketball skills.

The first thing I do to get ready for basketball camp is put on my basketball jersey and shorts.

Next I brush my teeth and wash my face.

Then I grab some fruit and eat before I leave the house.

The first thing we do at basketball camp is stretch.

The first basketball drill we do is the "Strong Fingers" drill. We can only dribble with the finger that "Coach Bear" told us to use. When we finish the first finger, we can use the next finger.

On the second drill, I had to sit in the chair and dribble three times. After that, I get up and dribble backwards. After I dribble backwards, I do two crossovers. Then, I did a between the legs and a spin move. After that, we had to dribble behind the back and shoot.

The next drill I did was pretty hard. I had to go up the court with only TWO dribbles! That means I had to push the ball in front of me twice to get up the whole court.

Next, I dribbled between my legs and took two steps to the left and shot the ball in the net.

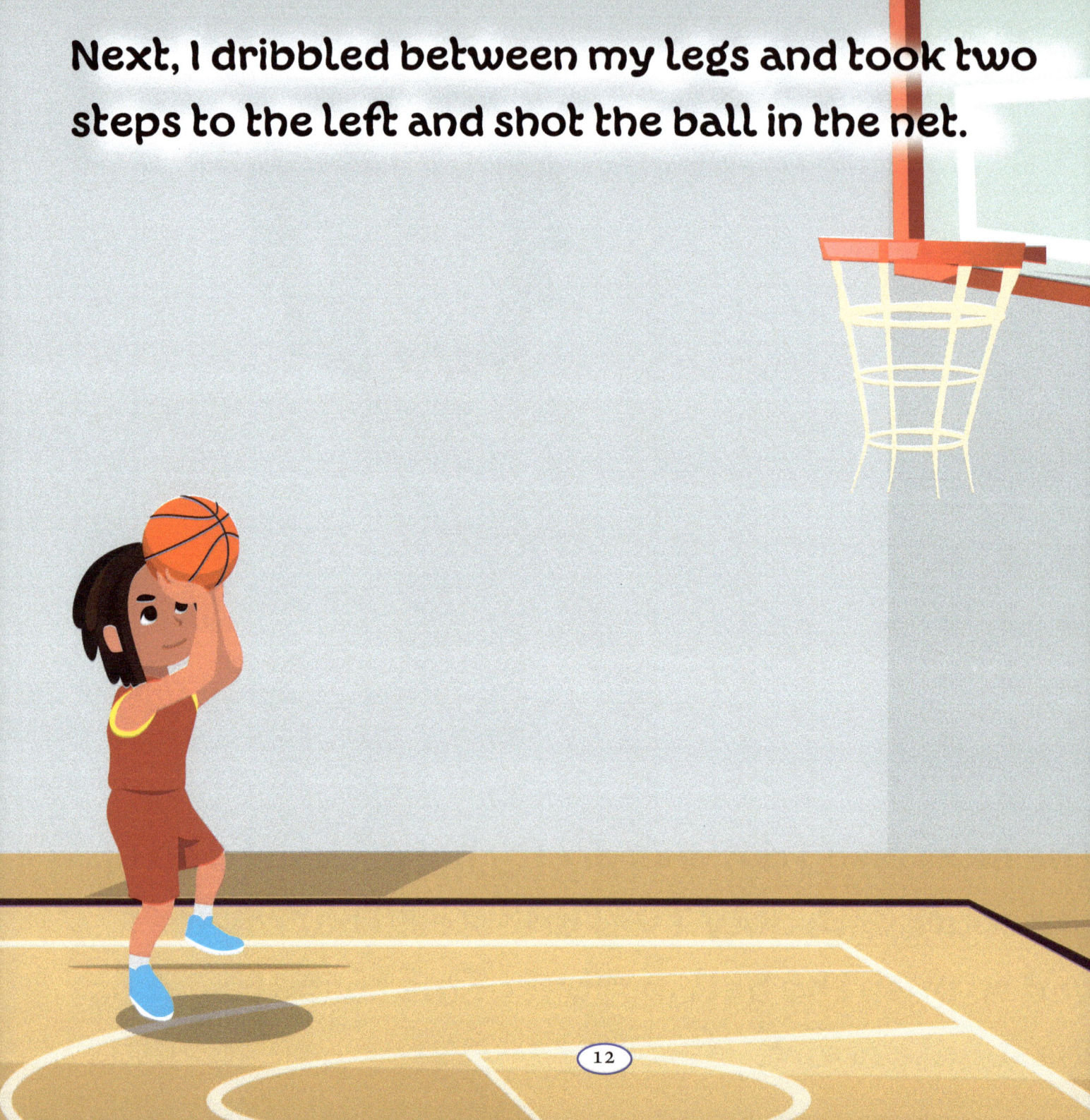

The next drill I did was also pretty hard. I had to do a front jab step dribble. Then, I had to do THREE crossovers! After that, I did a between the legs dribble. Then, I did ONE dribble to get up the court!

On the next drill, I had to come up the court in 4 dribbles! Then, I dribbled between the legs and took two steps to the right and shot the basketball in the hoop.

One thing I learned you have to do when you shoot the ball is hold your follow through and say "One one-thousand, Two one-thousand".

Another drill we did was called "layup lines". Layup lines are when we have two lines. One line for layups and the other for rebounds.

The second to last drill is "free throws". Free throws are shot at the line in front of the rim. Nobody can try to block your shot when you shoot a "free throw" so you have to make them, or you have to wait to get fouled again.

The last thing we do before we leave is "scrimmage". A scrimmage is a practice game! Whenever we scrimmage, I always score twice.

Before we leave, we stretch......AGAIN!

After camp is over, I always tell the coach "thanks for your time, Coach Bear!"

Then, me and my dad leave basketball camp and head home. We'll be back next week!